The 1990s

Britain in Pictures

The **1990s**
Britain in Pictures

PA Photos

AMMONITE
PRESS

First Published 2008 by
Ammonite Press
an imprint of AE Publications Ltd,
166 High Street, Lewes, East Sussex BN7 1XU

Text copyright Ammonite Press
Images copyright PA Photos
Copyright in the work Ammonite Press

ISBN 978-1-906672-15-7

British Cataloguing in Publication Data. A catalogue
record of this book is available from the British Library.

Series Editor: Paul Richardson
Editor: Huw Pryce
Picture research: PA Photos
Design: Gravemaker + Scott

Colour reproduction by GMC Reprographics
Printed by Colorprint, China

Page 2: Tony and Cherie
Blair in front of 10 Downing
Street.
2nd May, 1997

Page 5: The Prince of Wales
with The Spice Girls at the
end of the Royal Gala Show
celebrating 21 years of the
Prince's Trust in Manchester.
9th May, 1997

Page 6: The sea of flowers
continues to grow outside
the gates of Buckingham
Palace as thousands of
mourners from across Britain
and the world pay their last
respects to Diana, Princess
of Wales, before her funeral.
2nd September, 1997

Introduction

The archives of PA Photos yield a unique insight into Britain's recent past. Thanks to the science of photography we can view the 20th Century more accurately than any that came before, but it is thanks to news photography, and in particular the great news agency that is The Press Association, that we are able now to witness the events that made up life in Britain, not so long ago.

It is easy, looking back, to imagine a past neatly partitioned into clearly defined periods and dominated by landmarks: wars, political upheaval and economic trends. But the archive tells a different story: alongside the major events that constitute formal history are found the smaller things that had equal – if not greater – significance for ordinary people at the time. And while the photographers were working for that moment's news rather than posterity, the camera is an undiscriminating eye that records everything in its view: to modern eyes it is often the backgrounds of these pictures, not their intended subjects, that provide the greatest fascination. Likewise we see that Britain does not pass neatly from one period to another.

After the 1980s' headlong rush for home ownership, the new decade opened to falling property prices and negative equity for many householders. Bank base rates of over 15% added both to the misery of over-extended borrowers and to the mood of the times being generally depressed: the boom years were over. Margaret Thatcher resigns as Prime Minister following violent opposition to her Poll Tax, the world's biggest bank fraud – BCCI – exposed, attacks on Sterling force Britain to leave the ERM on Black Wednesday and Barings Bank fails. By the middle of the decade, belief in markets and money is thoroughly shaken and in 1997 the Conservatives suffer their worst election result of the century, losing to Labour after 18 years in office.

Then the country was rocked by news that caused greater, more widespread shock than any economic emergency: Diana, Princess of Wales, had died. Public reaction was overwhelming and sustained, an outpouring of grief that gathered momentum rather than subsiding. It has been said that events following Diana's death brought the monarchy closer to failing than it had been since the abdication crisis of the 1930s, but ultimately the effect was to unite rather than divide, and to signal that some things were more important than money.

The end of the millennium, however, was one issue on which Britain remained split: between those who anticipated a spectacular celebration, and those who predicted that chaos – a veritable apocalypse – would ensue from computers' feared inability to cope with a date in which the year began with the numeral '2'. As midnight approached on the 31st of December 1999 the nation held its collective breath and... nothing happened. The partygoers carried the day and the story of Britain in the 20th Century was complete.

Pete Waterman Limited, Hit
Factory products Sonia and
Big Fun.
2nd January, 1990

Facing page: Curator John
Simmons stands beside a
100 year old fallen black
pine, at Kew Gardens.
Almost 100 trees were
destroyed at the botanic
gardens in West London but
damage was nowhere near
as severe as the toll in the
1987 hurricane.
26th January, 1990

Margaret Thatcher toasts
Julie Goodyear and the
cast of 'Coronation Street'
during her visit to the Rover's
Return at Granada Television
Studios in Manchester.
26th January, 1990

Ben Elton, who co-wrote television's 'Blackadder' and 'The Young Ones', gets his own BBC TV show, 'Ben Elton - The Man from Auntie'.
6th February, 1990

Jubilant crowds outside
the South African embassy
in Trafalgar Square,
London, celebrating the
announcement that Nelson
Mandela is to be released.
10th February, 1990

Phil Collins and Annie Lennox after being named the Best British Male and Female Artists at The 1990 Brit Awards.
18th February, 1990

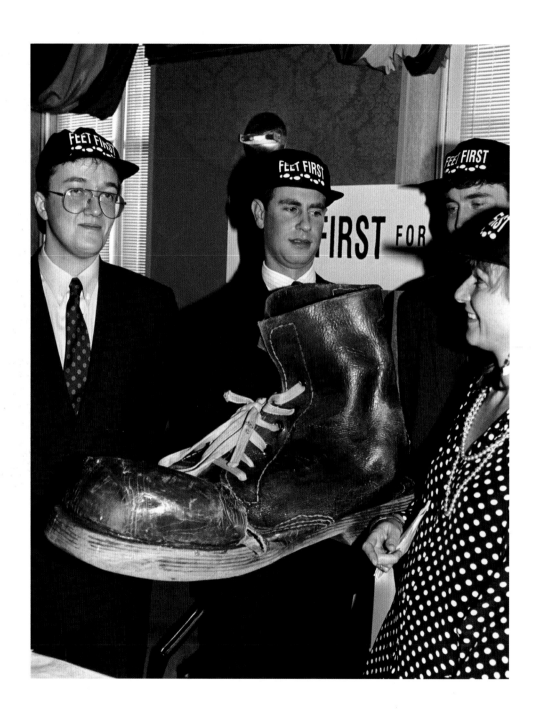

Prince Edward at the
launch of the Feet First
for Homeless People
campaign in London.
8th March, 1990

Luciano Pavarotti greets
the Queen Mother at a
gala performance of 'l'Elieir
d'Amore' at the Royal Opera
House, London.
21st March, 1990

Labour MP Tony Benn
addresses a demonstration
against the Poll Tax in
Trafalgar Square.
31st March, 1990

Poll Tax protesters in
Whitehall.
31st March, 1990

Portakabins in front of the
Higgs & Hill building burn as
rioting continues in London's
West End. Public reaction
to the Poll Tax leads to the
resignation of Prime Minister
Margaret Thatcher later in
the year.
1st April, 1990

Defiant, rioting prisoners on the rooftop of Strangeways Prison in Manchester. Prison officers are attacked and sex offenders on remand severely beaten as hooded prisoners armed with makeshift weapons rampage through the burning building.
4th April, 1990

TV Presenter Carol Smillie appearing at the 'Photography and Video '90' exhibition at the National Exhibition Centre in Birmingham.
5th April, 1990

Wrecked furniture on the
ground floor of D Wing at
Dartmoor Prison.
9th April, 1990

Night falls on the huge crowd
at the Nelson Mandela
concert at Wembley
Stadium.
16th April, 1990

Nelson Mandela speaking
to the tens of thousands
of fans gathered at
the concert in his honour.
17th April, 1990

Agriculture minister John Gummer and his four year old daughter Cordelia, tuck into a beef burger at the East Coast Boat Show in Ipswich, in a controversial attempt to calm public fears over the danger of BSE in British beef.

16th May, 1990

HMS 'Invincible' is
towed past the Thames
Barrier before berthing at
Greenwich.
13th June, 1990

'He's going to cry in a minute ...' England's Paul Gascoigne after defeat by West Germany in Turin.
4th July, 1990

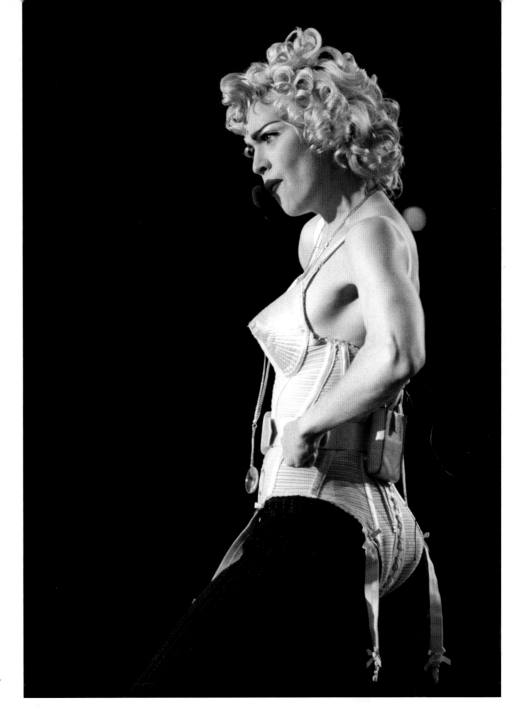

Madonna performs to a
crowd of 74,000 fans at
Wembley Stadium, London.
20th July, 1990

Members of the RAF Regiment, who will be manning the Rapier anti-aircraft missiles Britain is sending to Saudi Arabia, dressed in the primitive equipment intended to protect them from chemical weapons during the first Gulf War.
10th August, 1990

European Athletic
Championships, Split,
Yugoslavia, 100m Men's
Final. (L-R) Max Moriniere,
France; Linford Christie (first
place), Great Britain; Bruno
Marie Rose (third place),
France and John Regis,
Great Britain.
28th August, 1990

A Russian Antonov AN
225, the world's largest
flying aeroplane, over the
Swan public house during a
preview of the Farnborough
International Air Show.
2nd September, 1990

A rider on Whernside Fell,
during the Three Peaks
Cyclo-Cross Race.
29th September, 1990

Activists from the Animal Liberation Front following a raid on a laboratory owned by Boots the Chemist in London.
4th November, 1990

Facing page. Warrior tanks in the lines of armour and equipment waiting on the dockside at Bremerhaven before shipment to the Gulf.
30th September, 1990

The 800ft Canary Wharf Tower under construction in the London Docklands. The 50 storey structure contains 27,000 tonnes of British steel fastened by 500,000 bolts.
6th November, 1990

Challenger Chris Eubank (L)
trades blows with title holder
Nigel Benn (R) to win the
belt with a technical knock
out in the 9th round.
18th November, 1990

Tunnelling teams from
Britain and France celebrate
their arrival in Folkstone after
tunnellers broke through
to the French side creating
the first ground-based
connection to the continent
since the Ice Age.
20th November, 1990

Incoming Prime Minister
John Major and his wife
Norma, outside 10 Downing
Street.
28th November, 1990

Channel Four News presenters Jon Snow and Zeinab Badawi outside ITN's news studios in London's Grays Inn Road.
17th December, 1990

Huge waves swamp property on the promenade at Blackpool as gale force winds and a high tide combine to cause havoc for those living near the sea.
5th January, 1991

Royal Engineers of the 1st Armoured Division take cover as live mines explode during training in the Gulf, Saudi Arabia.
12th January, 1991

Members of the Jewish
community in Stamford
Hill, North London, discuss
missile attacks on Israel
by Iraq.
18th January, 1991

Crowds march from
Embankment, central
London, in protest against
the Gulf War.
26th January, 1991

A white van burns outside the Banqueting House in Whitehall after an attempted mortar attack on Downing Street.
7th February, 1991

Gary Lineker (L), and
Will Carling, captains of
England's national football
and Rugby Union teams, at
the launch of National No
Smoking day.
20th February, 1991

Firemen rescue residents
of Boroughbridge who were
trapped in their homes when
the River Ure flooded the
centre of the town.
24th February, 1991

The newly-freed Birmingham
Six outside the Old Bailey in
London. (L-R) William Power,
Richard McIlkenny, John
Walker, Gerry Hunter, Paddy
Hill and Hugh Callaghan.
14th March, 1991

Facing page: Prince William
and his mother, the Princess
of Wales, meet the crowds
as they leave Llandaff
Cathedral after the St
David's Day service.
1st March, 1991

The Princess of Wales
rides a chair-lift up the
Kriegerhorn with her sons
Prince William (L) and Prince
Harry, in Lech, Austria.
10th April, 1991

Tottenham Hotspur's Gary
Lineker (R) celebrates his
FA Cup winning goal against
Arsenal with Paul Allen (L).
14th April, 1991

Comedian and founder of the Hysteria Trust, Stephen Fry (bottom) in London to launch the third comedy and music gala for Aids charities. (L-R), Jennifer Saunders, Hugh Laurie, Emma Freud and Tony Slattery.
29th April, 1991

Paul and Linda McCartney in London to mark the launch of Linda's new vegetarian food range.
30th April, 1991

Andrew Lloyd Webber and his former wife, singer Sarah Brightman, at the Savoy Hotel in London, to celebrate her return to the London stage to star in 'The Music of Andrew Lloyd Webber' at the Prince Edward Theatre.
8th May, 1991

Wales beat Germany.
Ian Rush (R) out-sprints
Germany's Guido Buchwald
(L) to score the winning
goal in a UEFA Euro 1992
qualifying match.
5th June, 1991

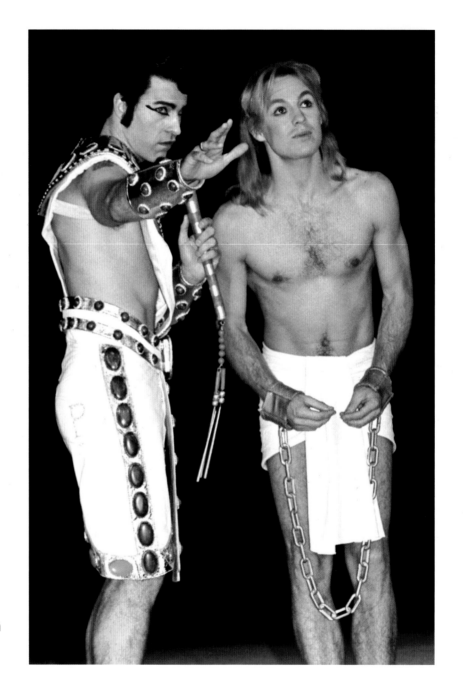

Jason Donovan (R) as
Joseph in 'Joseph and
the Amazing Technicolor
Dreamcoat', at the London
Palladium.
6th June, 1991

The completed Queen
Elizabeth II Bridge over the
River Thames at Dartford.
9th June, 1991

The Princess of Wales heads for the tape in the Mothers' Race at Wetherby School Sports Day at the Richmond Athletics Club. Prince Harry, her younger son, also took part in the events.

11th June, 1991

The Duchess of York, with her daughter Beatrice, and the Princess of Wales watch a flypast from the balcony at Buckingham Palace following the 'Trooping the Colour' ceremony.
15th June, 1991

Flashing lights, loud music and the sound of champagne corks popping mark the completion of the final section of the Channel Tunnel. The party took place 150ft below the seabed midway between England and France.

28th June, 1991

Athletics World Championships, Tokyo, Women's 3,000m Final. Britain's Yvonne Murray crashes to the floor after failing to win.
24th August, 1991

Athletics World
Championships, Tokyo,
Men's 4x400m Relay Final.
Kris Akabusi (L) crosses the
line ahead of USA's Antonio
Pettigrew to win gold for
Britain.
1st September, 1991

Holborn Job Centre.
The official national
unemployment total stands
at 2,450,689.
13th September, 1991

'Buckland' gives Rachel Brookes a closer look at the Upper Trout Hatchery during the cross country event at Burghley Horse Trials.
14th September, 1991

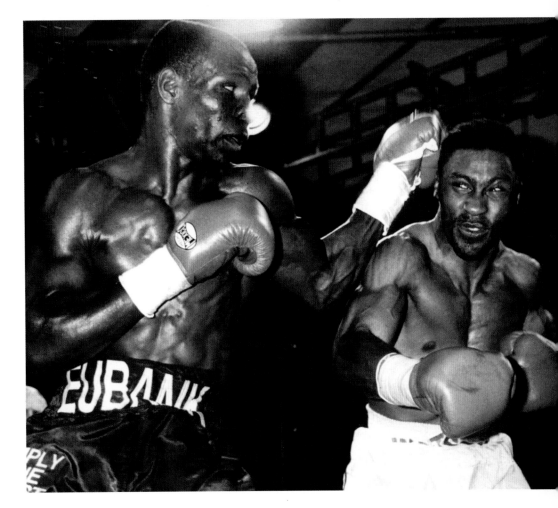

(L-R) Champion Chris Eubank dodges a right from challenger Michael Watson during the WBO Super Middleweight Championship. Eubank won the fight, which left Watson partially paralyzed and brain damaged after a 40 day coma and six brain operations.
21st September, 1991

Rugby World Cup. England's
Paul Ackford helps the team
to victory over Scotland in
the Semi-Final.
26th October, 1991

Blue Peter Christmas Appeal. (L-R) Diane-Louise Jordan, Yvette Fielding and John Leslie unveil details of the 1991 Blue Peter Christmas Appeal. The appeal involves the collection of everyday household items that have been discarded.

13th November, 1991

Gary Lineker scores the
equalizing goal against
Poland that takes England
through to the European
Championship Finals.
13th November, 1991

Freed Middle East hostage Terry Waite on arrival at RAF Lyneham. Waite was sent to Lebanon by the Archbishop of Canterbury to negotiate with Islamic Jihad for the return of hostages including John McCarthy. The Jihadis imprisoned him and he was held for a total of 1,763 days.

19th November, 1991

Prince Harry (C) arrives for a school carol concert at St Matthew's Church.
10th December, 1991

The Princess of Wales
visits India.
11th February, 1992

Rugby Union, Five Nations
Championship, England
v Wales, Twickenham.
England's Jason Leonard,
Dewi Morris and Martin
Bayfield are carried off by
fans after winning the Grand
Slam.
7th March, 1992

Former Prime Minister Margaret Thatcher is attacked by a woman wielding a bunch of flowers, during a walkabout in Marple Bridge in Stockport.
23rd March, 1992

Press photographers
wearing John Major masks
share an April Fool's
Day joke with the Prime
Minister as he speaks to the
crowd in Thornbury, North
Avon.
1st April, 1992

The scene of the bomb blast, at St Mary Axe in the City of London. Damage to buildings was so severe that they were later demolished. London's famous 'Gherkin' now stands on the site.
10th April, 1992

Elton John performs at
the Freddie Mercury
Tribute Concert
at Wembley, London.
20th April, 1992

Jim Bowen, presenter of hit
TV game show 'Bullseye'.
1st May, 1992

Boxer Frank Bruno frolics with TV personalities Michaela Strachen (L) and Lisa Maxwell outside the Dominion Theatre, where the threesome are appearing in the Children's Royal Variety Performance in aid of the NSPCC.

3rd May, 1992

The Queen watches
proceedings at the Royal
Windsor Horse Show.
16th May, 1992

Singer Kylie Minogue with Italian designer Gianni Versace at the opening of his new shop in London.
28th May, 1992

Ascot regular Mrs Gertrude Shilling arrives at the races wearing a sunflower creation.

16th June, 1992

Ulrika Jonsson and John
Fashanu host the new LWT
show 'Gladiators', recorded
at the NIA Birmingham.
19th June, 1992

Robots at work on the Rover
200 Series production line at
Longbridge.
15th July, 1992

Racing driver Nigel Mansell
with the Nottingham Forest
FC team and manager Brian
Clough.
31st July, 1992

Barcelona Olympic Games. Linford Christie, Great Britain, celebrates winning the Men's 100m event.
1st August, 1992

Sterling dealers on the trading floor of Nat West's foreign exchange department, Bishopsgate, City of London, as Sterling remains in the danger zone on Europe's Exchange Rate Mechanism.
2nd August, 1992

Facing page: Coxed Pair, (L-R) Greg Searle, Jonathan Searle and cox Garry Herbert celebrate winning gold at the Barcelona Olympics.
2nd August, 1992

Barcelona Olympic Games.
Sally Gunnell wins gold in
the 400m Hurdles.
05 August, 1992

New age travellers at
a police road block in
Winchester.
9th August, 1992

Dealers trading in Sterling
at the London International
Financial Futures and
Options Exchange (LIFFE).
21st September, 1992

(L-R) Visibly exhausted Gerhard Berger, Nigel Mansell and Ayrton Senna on the winners' podium at the Portuguese Grand Prix.
1st October, 1992

Roy Castle and
a giant cigarette mark
the country's first ever
Ashtray Amnesty Day.
7th October, 1992

The Prince of Wales takes a close look at some of the specimen trees at the Royal Duchy Nursery at Lostwithiel in Cornwall.

13th November, 1992

Harry Secombe (L) and Roy
Castle celebrate Christmas
together for ITV's 'Highway'
programme.
13th November, 1992

Norman Tebbit (L) and
Timmy Mallett at the launch
of the Give the Gift of Sight
appeal, to collect spare
spectacles for distribution to
needy adults and children in
third world countries.
17th November, 1992

Firemen at Windsor Castle
tackle a fierce fire, which
threatens one of the greatest
collections of art in the
world.
20th November, 1992

Facing page: The stricken oil
tanker 'Braer', aground off
the Shetland coast.
6th January, 1993

Lloyd Honeyghan beats
Mickey Hughes to become
the Commonwealth Light-
Middleweight Boxing
Champion in Brentwood,
Essex.
30th January, 1993

England v India, Second
Test Match, Madras.
England's Robin Smith
just makes his ground and
avoids being run out.
13th February, 1993

'The Darling Buds of May' returns for a third series. (L-R) David Jason (Pop Larkin), Abigail Rokison (Primrose), Phillip Franks (Charley) and Pam Ferris (Ma Larkin).

19th February, 1993

Chris Evans, host of Channel Four's 'Big Breakfast', will present a Saturday morning show on Virgin Radio.
24th February, 1993

Eric Cantona in the FA Carling Premiership, Manchester United v Aston Villa at Old Trafford.
14th March, 1993

The Queen at the Royal Air Force's 75th Anniversary celebration at RAF Marham, Norfolk. Rain forces the cancellation of the flypast and cuts proceedings short.
1st April, 1993

Outside the Hong Kong Shanghai Bank in Bishopsgate, City of London following a massive bomb blast. A crater in the left foreground marks the seat of the explosion.
26th April, 1993

Outgoing Nottingham Forest manager Brian Clough surrounded by well-wishing fans after his last game in charge at the City ground.
1st May, 1993

Noel Edmonds, (L) with BBC
One controller Alan Yentob
after Edmonds signs a
contract, reputedly worth £10
million, for a new series of
'Noel's House Party'.
13th May, 1993

(L-R) Journalists Richard Pendlebury (The Daily Mail), Charlie Rae (Today), Philip Sherwell (Daily Telegraph), Gervaise Webb (Evening Standard), Rob Jonson (Daily Express) and James Hardy (Press Association) at the Westerplatte war memorial in Poland.
20th May, 1993

A mass meeting of the workforce from the threatened Swan Hunter shipyard gathers outside the yard at Wallsend near Newcastle.
26th May, 1993

The Queen and Prince of
Wales at Epsom on the 40th
anniversary of the Queen's
Coronation.
2nd June, 1993

Actor Richard Wilson as Victor Meldrew on location in Portugal to film the BBC One feature-length 'One Foot in the Algarve' Christmas special.
3rd June, 1993

The Holbeck Hall Hotel in
Scarborough after a massive
landslip. Scarborough
Borough Council is
subsequently held liable for
the destruction of the hotel
after it was found to be in
breach of its duty of care to
maintain the supporting land.
8th June, 1993

The Duke and Duchess of York enjoy sports day at Upton House School, Windsor, which is attended by their daughter Princess Beatrice.
23rd June, 1993

The tall ships leave the
River Tyne for the start
of the Cutty Sark Race at
Newcastle.
17th July, 1993

Prince Harry visits the
barracks of the Light
Dragoons in Hanover,
Germany.
29 July, 1993

Female impersonator Paul
O'Grady, alias Lily Savage,
at home in South London.
16th August, 1993

Rupert Murdoch at the launch of Sky Television's new multi-channel package giving viewers a choice of more than 20 channels.
1st September, 1993

The demolition of two 19
storey blocks of flats at
Queen Elizabeth Square,
Gorbals in Glasgow, billed
as the biggest controlled
explosion in Europe since
the Second World War.
12th September, 1993

Luciano Pavarotti appears
on a giant screen during his
open air concert at Leeds
Castle.
29th September, 1993

Preparations for the funeral of Sir Matt Busby. Arthur Ludden, a Manchester United fan for over 60 years and blind for the past five, touches the scarves at the shrine of tributes at Old Trafford.

26th January, 1994

Model Naomi Campbell wearing a wedding dress made from newspapers and dollar bills as part of the New Renaissance collection at the Harvey Nichols and Perrier New Generation Designers Show.
24th February, 1994

'Flax', the last pit pony working in a British colliery, is led away from Ellington Pit by farrier Keith Adams.
24th February, 1994

Jayne Torvill and Christopher
Dean dance the 'Bolero'
at the end of the Winter
Olympics at Lillehammer.
26th February, 1994

'Eastenders' stars (L-R)
Bill Treacher, Wendy
Richard and Michael
French celebrate
the announcement that
the show will be transmitted
three times a week.
9th March, 1994

West Indies v England, Fifth
Test. Brian Lara kisses the
wicket that gave him his
record breaking test innings
of 364 not out.
18th April, 1994

Farmer Mitch Atkinson
tending his sheep under
the shadow of the huge
'Golf Ball' radomes, at the
Fylingdales US early warning
base, North Yorkshire.
21st April, 1994

Controversial British artist, Damien Hirst, with 'Away from the Flock', a dead lamb suspended in formaldehyde, which features in an exhibition at London's Serpentine Gallery. Hirst, 28, achieved notoriety with sculptures that concentrate on putrefaction.
3rd May, 1994

The Queen and the Duke of
Edinburgh travel on the new
Eurostar train.
6th May, 1994

Facing page: Actor Hugh Grant and Elizabeth Hurley arrive for the charity premiere of 'Four Weddings and a Funeral'. 'That dress was a favour from Versace because I couldn't afford to buy one. His people told me they didn't have any evening wear, but there was one item left in their press office.' Says Hurley of the event. 'That dress' lands her the position as the face of Estée Lauder.

11th May, 1994

Prime Minister John Major checks his watch as President Bill Clinton addresses the media at Chequers.
5th June, 1994

Irish actor Pierce Brosnan
is named as the new James
Bond.
8th June, 1994

Colin Jackson in the
110m Hurdles heats at
the European Athletics
Championship, Helsinki.
11th August, 1994

Jürgen Klinsmann celebrates
scoring his first goal for
Tottenham Hotspur against
Sheffield Wednesday.
20th August, 1994

Damon Hill's Williams
Renault drives over a graffiti
tribute to the late Ayrton
Senna at Spa during the
Belgian Grand Prix.
29th August, 1994

A Republican paints 'IRA' on the wall of Springfield Road police station in West Belfast, where crowds of nationalists gather as the IRA ceasefire comes into effect at midnight.
1st September, 1994

The first National Lottery poster bearing the slogan 'It Could Be You'. The posters are the first stage of a huge promotional campaign in the run-up to the lottery launch.
27th October, 1994

'National Lottery' presenters (L-R) Gordon Kennedy, Noel Edmonds and Anthea Turner with the machine that will make someone a millionaire when the first ever draw takes place.
18th November, 1994

The Prince of Wales eats
a bowl of jellied eels at
Surrey Street Market,
Croydon. Surrey Street
was established in the
13th Century and is one
of London's oldest street
markets.
29th November, 1994

Alan Johnson, with children
Maria 14, Louise 11, and
Emma 3, make it through
water, sometimes up
to five feet deep, from
their marooned home at
Sandhurst, near Gloucester.
1st February, 1995

Frantic bidding on the floor of the London International Financial Futures and Options Exchange (LIFFE) after the Bank of England raised interest rates by 0.5% to 6.76% in a bid to cool the economy.

2nd February, 1995

Blur – (L-R) Alex James,
Dave Rowntree, Damon
Albarn and Graham Coxon
– win a Brit Award for Top
British Artists of the year.
21st February, 1995

Supermodel Kate Moss signs copies of her book, 'Kate', at London's Virgin Megastore.
20th April, 1995

The Queen, The Queen
Mother and Princess
Margaret watch a procession
of vintage planes over
Buckingham Palace to mark
the 50th anniversary of VE
(Victory in Europe) Day.
8th May, 1995

The Queen uses a Leica camera to photograph the Duke of Edinburgh as he competes in the Dressage section of the Carriage Driving Championships at the Royal Windsor Horse Show.

12th May, 1995

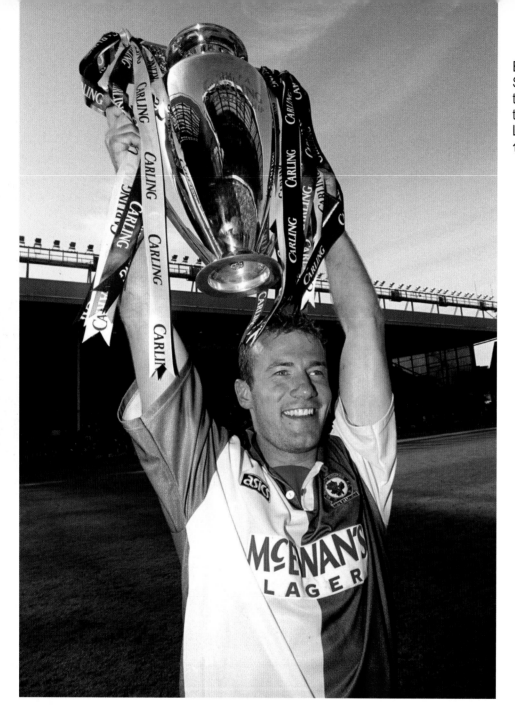

Blackburn Rovers' Alan Shearer celebrates with the Carling Premiership trophy after their defeat of Liverpool.

14 May, 1995

Rugby Union World Cup, South Africa. (L-R) England's Mike Catt, Kyran Bracken, Neil Back and Richard West playing on the beach in Durban.

25th May, 1995

David Coulthard's Williams-McLaren faces the traffic as Gerhard Berger's Ferrari is lifted into the air during a snarl-up at the start of the Monaco Grand Prix.

28th May, 1995

John Daly celebrates his unexpected win at the Open Golf Championship with his wife, as a streaker races off in the background.
23rd July, 1995

The Prince and Princess of Wales with sons Prince William (R) and Prince Harry, attending the VJ (Victory in Japan) Day commemorations at Buckingham Palace.
19th August, 1995

(L-R) Party leaders John Major (Conservative), Paddy Ashdown (Liberal Democrats) and Tony Blair (Labour) talk before a 'Beating the Retreat' ceremony in London, during the VJ (Victory in Japan) Day anniversary.

20th August, 1995

PC World, Croydon.
Microsoft's Windows 95
operating system goes on
sale at midnight across the
country.
23rd August, 1995

The end of the summer arrives on Blackpool beach as the scorching weather of the previous few weeks comes to an abrupt end.
24th August, 1995

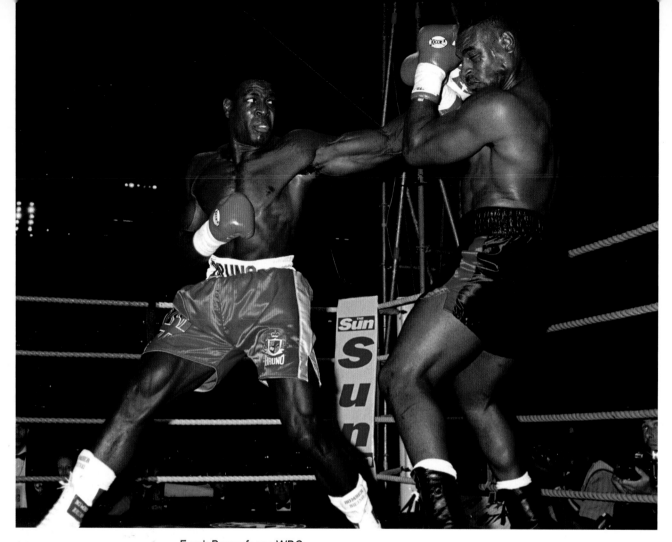

Frank Bruno faces WBC
Heavyweight Champion
Oliver McCall at Wembley
Stadium.
2nd September, 1995

Newly crowned WBC
Heavyweight Champion
Frank Bruno proudly shows
off his world title belt with his
daughter Rachel in London,
after defeating Oliver McCall.
3rd September, 1995

Jockeys Frankie Dettori (L) and Willie Carson get to grips with the country's smallest and largest breeds, a Shire horse called 'Brookfield Albion' (L) and 'Chico', a 20 year old Falabella, at the launch of the Ascot Festival.
5th September, 1995

Stena Sealink's 'Challenger' ferry runs aground just outside the French port of Calais.
20th September, 1995

Tony Blair (R) takes part in a ball-heading contest with Newcastle United boss Kevin Keegan in Brighton during a break in the Labour party conference.
2nd October, 1995

Workmen reconstructing the Globe Theatre in London on its original site on the South Bank of the Thames. The Arts Council comes under fire for giving the bulk of its National Lottery handout to just two London venues, with £12.4 million going to the Globe project and nearly £30 million going to the Sadler's Wells dance theatre.

16th October, 1995

Lorraine Chase helps launch
easyJet's new low-cost
service to Edinburgh and
Glasgow from Luton Airport.
The airline aims to fly
passengers to Scotland for
less than the cost of a pair
of jeans.
18th October, 1995

Housewife superstar
Dame Edna Everage visits
'Coronation Street'.
23rd October, 1995

John Galliano, recently appointed chief designer for Givenchy, celebrates with a model wearing one of his creations after being named British Designer of the Year at the British Fashion Awards. It is the second year running and third time in the event's history that Galliano has won the award.
24th October, 1995

Brian Conley rehearsing on
stage for his portrayal of
screen legend Al Jolson at
the Victoria Palace theatre.
24th October, 1995

Crowds gather outside
Buckingham Palace to catch
a glimpse of their idol, Cliff
Richard, as he arrives to
collect his knighthood. Three
women from Gloucester
(green jumpers, C) have
been waiting at the palace
since 3:00am to get a good
view.
25th October, 1995

'Coronation Street' actor Johnny Briggs, who plays Mike Baldwin, samples the giant birthday cake to celebrate the soap's forthcoming 35th anniversary, at the Granada TV studios in Manchester.
31st October, 1995

Former Manchester United soccer stars (L-R) Denis Law, Bobby Charlton and George Best at the launch of Sky Sports Gold, a satellite and cable channel specialising in classic sporting moments.
31st October, 1995

Hundreds of telephones arrive at the BT Tower in London, ready for the annual Children In Need Appeal. The Tower is nerve-centre for the appeal, dealing with 300,000 calls from people wanting to pledge money.
19th November, 1995

(R) Colin McRae and co-driver Derek Ringer celebrate their World Rally Championship victory at Chester Racecourse.
22nd November, 1995

Television presenter
Jonathan Ross (L)
buttonholed by alternative
TV pundit Dennis Pennis
at the Cafe Royal, London.
The pair are attending
the first National Perudo
Tournament, a recreation of
the ancient Peruvian game,
Dudo.

6th December, 1995

The **1990s** Britain in Pictures **165**

Manchester United's Eric
Cantona volleys in the
equalising goal against
Sheffield Wednesday.
9th December, 1995

Filey's fishing boats lie under
a heavy covering of snow.
28th December, 1995

Bringing home the haggis
for Burns Night, the 200th
anniversary of the Bard's
birth. Scots all over world
will be toasting their hero
with the traditional delicacy,
which consists of offal,
suet and oats stuffed into a
sheep's stomach.
24th January, 1996

Michael Jackson swings out over the audience in a crane hoist while performing his hit 'Earthsong' at a star-studded Brit award ceremony at London's Earl's Court. The performance descends into farce when Pulp's Jarvis Cocker invades the stage in protest at the content of the stage show.
19th February, 1996

Take That at the Brit Awards.
Their cover of the Bee Gees
hit 'How Deep is Your Love',
the last single to be released
following the band's decision
to split, has gone straight in
at Number One in the pop
charts.
19th February, 1996

The mangled remains of
the 171 London bus blown
apart by an IRA bomb in the
Aldwych, London.
20th February, 1996

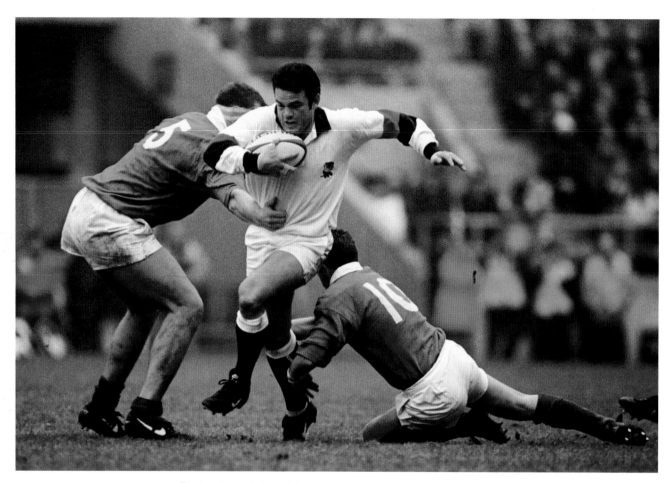

England's captain Will Carling tackled by (L) Ireland's Jeremy Davidson and David Humphreys during the Five Nations Championship match at Twickenham.
16th March, 1996

Animal rights activists demonstrate outside the Ministry of Agriculture in London as government ministers and scientists meet to consider how to solve the crisis in the British beef industry caused by the discovery that Bovine Spongiform Encephalopathy - Mad Cow Disease - has crossed into humans. The Government is considering the slaughter of four million cattle over 30 months old.
25th March, 1996

RUC Officers under a petrol
bomb attack on the Ormeau
Road, Belfast, when an
Apprentice Boys' march
is prevented from walking
through a Catholic area of
the city.
8th April, 1996

Comedy duo Vic Reeves (L) and Bob Mortimer at the BAFTA ceremony in London to collect their award for 'The Smell of Reeves and Mortimer'.
21st April, 1996

Damon Hill wins the San
Marino Grand Prix.
5th May, 1996

Frank Biela's Audi leads the chasing pack at the start of the British Touring Car Championship at Oulton Park, during a year widely considered as the golden age of Super Touring.
27th May, 1996

Euro 96, Group A, England
v Scotland. England's
Paul Gascoigne (on floor)
re-enacts the infamous
'dentist's chair incident' with
Teddy Sheringham (L) after
scoring the second goal.
15th June, 1996

The scene of total
devastation in Manchester
city centre caused by
Britain's biggest mainland
terrorist bomb explosion.
The Victorian post box
which survived the blast
now carries a small plaque
marking its extraordinary
history for future generations
to see.
16th June, 1996

Stuart Pearce exorcises
the ghosts of penalties past
as he celebrates scoring
in the penalty shoot-out to
decide the Euro 96 quarter
final clash against Spain, at
Wembley.

22nd June, 1996

Dejected Gareth Southgate
holds his head in his hands
after missing the final
penalty against Germany.
26th June, 1996

Princess Diana visits the
Mortimer Market Centre in
London, a clinic for HIV/AIDS
patients.
27 June, 1996

Nelson Mandela, President of South Africa, and the Queen ride along the Mall on the first full day of his state visit to Britain.
9th July, 1996

RUC officers stand ready
for any violence as 10,000
Orangemen arrive at
Drumcree to support the
Portadown Orange Lodges.
11th July, 1996

A Protestant Orange Lodge
band marches on Belfast's
Ormeau Road while Catholic
residents are barricaded
in their own streets behind
security vehicles.
12th July, 1996

Olympic Games, Atlanta:
Matthew Pinsent and Steve
Redgrave of Great Britain
win the gold medal for the
Coxless Pairs rowing event.
27th July, 1996

Keith Flint of The Prodigy joins the crowd during the band's performance at Knebworth, supporting Oasis.

10th August, 1996

Sinn Fein President Gerry
Adams addresses a rally
outside Belfast City Hall.
10th August, 1996

Liall Bolens, 12 (L) and
Chris McQuade, 11 (R) play
football on Methley Terrace,
Leeds, after Transport 2000
and the local residents turfed
the street at the launch of
their 'Streets for People'
campaign, designed to
reduce the amount of traffic
in residential streets.
16th August, 1996

Pulp's Jarvis Cocker
sings to more than 35,000
fans at Hylands Park in
Chelmsford, Essex. Country
roads around the two-day
festival site jammed as
crowds braved the heat at
the summer outdoor music
extravaganza.
17th August, 1996

Chris Boardman of Great Britain during his world record breaking ride in the first round of the Individual Pursuit on the first day of the World Track Cycling Championships in Manchester. He took nearly six seconds off the record.

28th August, 1996

Artist Antony Gormley overseeing the installation of his 'Field for the British Isles' work at the Hayward Gallery, London. The 40,000 tiny terracotta figures will fill an entire gallery.
13th September, 1996

Doncaster: Frankie Dettori
dismounts spectacularly
after winning the St Leger on
'Shantou'.
14th September, 1996

Television commentator
Murray Walker in the
Williams garage at the
Estoril circuit for the
Portuguese Grand Prix.
19th September, 1996

25 Cromwell Street, Gloucester. Demolition is due to start on the former home of serial sex murderers Fred and Rosemary West.
4th October, 1996

Michael Schumacher
and Mika Hakkinen pour
champagne over the new
World Champion Damon Hill
at the end of the Japanese
Grand Prix.
13th October, 1996

Liam Gallagher and fiancée Patsy Kensit arrive at the first screening of the film 'The Rolling Stones Rock and Roll Circus' at the London Astoria.
15th October, 1996

Michael Flatley, the 'Lord
of the Dance'.
12th November, 1996

Winner Chris Evans (C),
Top Channel 4/BBC2
Entertainment Presenter, is
hugged by award presenters
Gaby Roslin (L) and Zoe
Ball at the British Comedy
Awards at the London
Television Centre.
1st December, 1996

Coventry City goalkeeper
Steve Ogrizovic (L) saves
a diving header from Allan
Nielsen of Tottenham
Hotspur (R).
7th December, 1996

Diana, Princess of Wales, touring a minefield in body armour to see for herself the carnage mines cause, during her visit to Angola.

15th January, 1997

Westminster City Council bans feeding the birds in Trafalgar Square in an attempt to cut the population.
17th January, 1997

A butcher's display greets
the Prince of Wales' visit
to Grainger Market in
Newcastle.
24th January, 1997

Pictures of the victims are carried through a crowd of thousands at Free Derry Corner on the 25th anniversary march for 'Bloody Sunday'.
2nd February, 1997

Facing page: Vivienne Westwood makes a triumphant return to Britain for the catwalk show of her Autumn/Winter collection. It is the first time Miss Westwood has displayed a collection at London Fashion Week since 1990.
23rd February, 1997

Lead singer of Kula Shaker, Crispian Mills, makes a speech in acceptance of the band's Best British Newcomer award, at the Brits ceremony, in London.
24th February, 1997

The Spice Girls at the Brit
Awards in London, where
they scooped awards for
Best British Video and Best
Single.
24th February, 1997

Geri Halliwell and Victoria Adams of the Spice Girls at the Brits.
24th February, 1997

Environmental campaigner Swampy, on the site of the proposed second runway at Manchester airport, announces he will be standing in the General Election. The man dubbed the most famous eco-warrior in the country has joined campaigners protesting at the £172 million development.
31st March, 1997

'Hale Bopp', the brightest
comet seen for over a
century, above Glastonbury
Tor.
3rd April, 1997

Tony Blair relaxes at his home in Islington, North London.
8th April, 1997

A smoke bomb is thrown
into the entrance of Downing
Street and distress flares let
off as hundreds of protesters
harangue police standing
behind barriers during a
march to support sacked
Liverpool dockers.
12th April, 1997

Leicester City's Steve Claridge blasts the ball past Middlesbrough's goalkeeper Ben Roberts to score the winning goal in the Coca Cola Cup Final replay.
16 April, 1997

New Prime Minister Tony Blair and his wife, Cherie, greet well-wishers as they walk into Downing Street. Labour won the general election with a landslide victory, leaving the Tories with their poorest result since 1832.
2nd May, 1997

A replica of Captain Cook's
ship 'The Endeavour' arrives
at the original's home port
of Whitby. The ship was
built in Freemantle, Australia
to commemorate Cook's
historic voyage.
9th May, 1997

'Dolly' the sheep, the world's first ever cloned animal, is sheared by world champion shearer Geordie Bayne from Hawick at the Roslin Institute, near Edinburgh, to raise money for the Cystic Fibrosis charity.
20th May, 1997

British Lions' Tour of South Africa. Jeremy Guscott celebrates at the end of the second test after the Lions' victory.
28th June, 1997

Fans watching the Tim
Henman and Richard
Krajicek match on the
video screen at Court One,
Wimbledon.
2nd July, 1997

Noel Gallagher of the band
Oasis and his new wife
Meg talk to Tony Blair at a
Downing Street reception.
Meg Gallagher is wearing
an outfit by designer Rifat
Ozbek.
30th July, 1997

A member of the disabled
people's Direct Action
Network (DAN) lies
handcuffed to a number 12
bus near Downing Street
during a demonstration
calling for all public transport
to be accessible to the
disabled by the year 2007.
22nd August, 1997

The Notting Hill Carnival,
Europe's largest street
festival: two million are
expected to take part in the
celebrations.
25th August, 1997

The bearer party of Welsh Guardsmen carry the coffin of Diana, Princess of Wales, out of Westminster Abbey.
6th September, 1997

Facing page: Earl Spencer lays flowers on the island in the grounds of the family home at Althorp, Northamptonshire, where his sister Diana, Princess of Wales, is buried.
8th September, 1997

The clear-up at the site of
the Southall rail crash after a
Great Western express train
ploughed into a goods train
leaving six dead and more
than 160 injured.
20th September, 1997

Kate Moss (second R), Alek Wek (L) and Mick Jagger's daughter Jade (R) wait behind the scenes of the Matthew Williamson show at London Fashion Week.
26th September, 1997

(L-R) Vic Reeves, John Thomson, Paul Whitehouse, Bob Mortimer, Arabella Weir, Ulrika Jonsson and Charlie Higson announce a live performance of 'Shooting Stars' and 'The Fast Show' to take place at the London Labatt's Apollo, Hammersmith.
1st October, 1997

London's Docklands, as construction work begins on the £580 million Millennium Dome.
10th October, 1997

Attracting almost as much
media attention as the real
thing, Spice Girls dolls
are launched at the British
Association of Toy Retailers'
fair in London.
16th October, 1997

The Royal Yacht 'Britannia' makes her final trip up the River Thames, through the Thames Barrier, at the end of a national farewell tour of the UK.

13th November, 1997

Ash Street, Salford
celebrates Barbie's Pink
Month. Barbie's makers,
Mattel, are giving a
five figure sum to local
community groups in return
for the permission given
by the 70 residents of the
traditional Victorian street to
temporarily transform their
homes.
17th November, 1997

Liam Gallagher, lead singer
with Oasis, at Wembley
Arena.
16th December, 1997

The seafront in Weston
Super Mare, Somerset
during heavy storms.
4th January, 1998

Robbie Williams and Tom
Jones perform at the
Brit Awards ceremony at
London's Docklands Arena.
9th February, 1998

Locals gather to watch as the wings are attached to Antony Gormley's controversial new north of England landmark – a gigantic steel sculpture, entitled 'Angel of the North', by the A1 Gateshead by-pass in Tyneside.
15th February, 1998

'Strapper', a Jack Russell,
becomes the David Bailey
of the dog world, as a row of
obedient whippets have their
picture taken in London in
the lead up to Crufts.
19th February, 1998

Vivienne Westwood's
Autumn/Winter 98/99
collection at London
Fashion Week.
21st February, 1998

(L-R) Wales' Mike Voyle, Gareth Llewellyn and England's Martin Johnson in the line-out, during the Five Nations Championship, England v Wales match. England won by 60 points to 26.
21st February, 1998

Prime Minister Tony Blair
and his Deputy, John
Prescott, view a model of the
Millennium Dome.
24th February, 1998

Jack Docherty and Sara Cox celebrate the first anniversary of Channel 5, at the company's London office.
30th March, 1998

Newcastle United's Alan
Shearer celebrates scoring
against Sheffield to send
Newcastle through to the FA
Cup Final.
05 April, 1998

A Spitfire Mk V in formation
with a Spitfire Mk IX (C)
and a Spitfire XIV (Top)
over Cambridgeshire. The
three aircraft are part of
the Spitfire Air Show at
the Imperial War Museum,
Duxford.
30th April, 1998

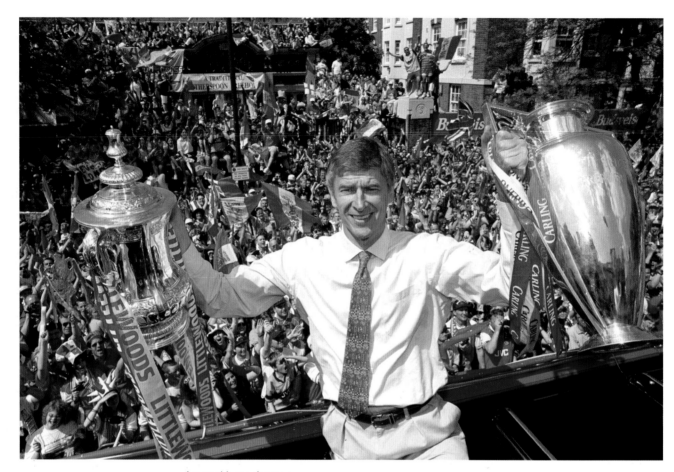

Arsenal boss Arsene
Wenger with the FA and
League Cups as the team
take a victory tour from the
Highbury ground to Islington
Town Hall to celebrate their
cup double.
17th May, 1998

(L-R) Ian Broudie of The Lightning Seeds and comedians Frank Skinner and David Baddiel announce their new version of the footballing hit 'Three Lions' to coincide with the 1998 World Cup.
22nd May, 1998

England goalkeeper Nigel
Martyn dives to save
a penalty from Belgium's
Enzo Scifo.
29th May, 1998

Something to celebrate at last for the British coal mining industry: the Government announces proposals to protect the remaining working pits with a number of measures including restrictions on the construction of more gas fired power stations and curbs on open cast developments.

25th June, 1998

Rivers of mud at the
Glastonbury Festival.
27th June, 1998

Early morning at the
Glastonbury festival.
28th June, 1998

Pete Sampras wins
the Men's Singles final
at Wimbledon.
05 July, 1998

Members of the Portadown Lodge
of the Orange Order are stopped
on leaving Drumcree Church
by a roadblock preventing them
completing the traditional route
of the annual march down the
nationalist Garvaghy Road.
5th July, 1998

One of London's homeless
and his belongings.
20th July, 1998

Anthony McPartlin (L) and
Declan Donnelly meet Cat
Deeley, co-presenter of new
Saturday morning TV series
'SMTV Live'.
27th July, 1998

England's Darren Gough (C) celebrates after taking the wicket of South Africa's Makhaya Ntini (L), to win the Fifth Cornhill Test, and the series, for England at Headingly.
10th August, 1998

David Coulthard signs
autographs after spinning off
during practice laps for the
Hungarian Grand Prix.
15th August, 1998

Seventeenth European
Athletics Championships,
Budapest. Great Britain's
Denise Lewis celebrates
after winning the Heptathlon.
22nd August, 1998

The last day of the last week of Dickie Bird's umpiring career. Dickie Bird relaxes with a cup of tea in the inner sanctum of the umpires' room at Headingley. The start of the Yorkshire v Warwickshire game was delayed by rain.
9th September, 1998

Caricaturist Gerald Scarfe
unveils his new creation,
based on Prime Minister
Tony Blair, at the National
Portrait Gallery.
1st October, 1998

Tony and Cherie Blair near
the end of an official visit to
China.
8th October, 1998

Eton College students
look down on the Eton
Wall Game from
the eponymous wall.
28th November, 1998

The Queen Mother at
London's Theatre Royal
where she has unveiled a
specially commissioned
statue by Angela Conner,
of her old friend playwright
Noel Coward.
8th December, 1998

RUC riot police under attack as Nationalist youths hijack a van and set it on fire during an Apprentice Boys' parade in Londonderry.
12th December, 1998

The Millennium Dome in
Greenwich stands against
the London skyline. The
Queen is to attend the
opening ceremony.
29th December, 1998

'The Angel of the North' in Newcastle with sculptor Antony Gormley. The sculptor won an award for visual arts at the 1999 'South Bank Show' awards.
21st January, 1999

A Mini designed by fashion designer Paul Smith, for a competition to celebrate the car which was first unveiled 40 years earlier.

8th February, 1999

A sculpture by Anglo-French artist Pierre Vivant in East London. Made from 75 sets of specially-manufactured traffic lights finished in green, it is the result of an international competition organised by the Public Arts Commissions Agency.

9th February, 1999

David Beckham (L) bends a
free kick through the French
wall during a friendly match.
10th February, 1999

Annie Lennox of the
Eurythmics performs at
the Brit Awards. The band,
reunited for the occasion,
are presented with the
Outstanding Contribution to
British Music award.
16th February, 1999

Wales v Ireland in the Five
Nations, Ireland win 29-23.
20th February, 1999

Leicester's Darren Garforth struggles with his headband.
27th March, 1999

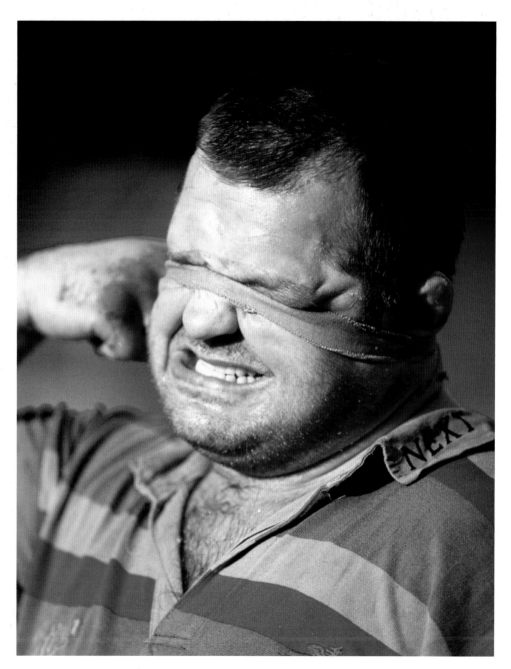

Facing page: Grace Jones models one of the hats created by designer Philip Treacy, at London Fashion Week.
21st February, 1999

The Prince of Wales talks to
14 year old Lewis Hamilton,
who is sponsored by
McLaren's driver support
programme, at their Formula
One factory in Woking.
31st March, 1999

Concorde touches down at Filton, Bristol, 30 years to the day after the first of its type took its maiden flight from Filton to Fairford. Plans to stop off at the former test site at RAF Fairford were cancelled because the base is being used by US bombers in the Kosovan conflict.

9th April, 1999

Wigan Athletic's winning goal scorer Paul Rogers is the victim of a practical joke as he celebrates beating Millwall for the Auto Windscreens Shield.
18th April, 1999

At least five people are injured when a bomb explodes in Brick Lane at the centre of the capital's Bangladeshi community, exactly a week after a similar bomb in Brixton.
25th April, 1999

Morris dancers at the
May Day celebrations at
Rochester in Kent.
1st May, 1999

Manchester United's Ole Gunnar Solskjaer celebrates the winning goal against Bayern Munich with Dwight Yorke and Ronny Johnsen.
26th May, 1999

Manchester United celebrate
their win in the UEFA
Champions League against
Bayern Munich.
26th May, 1999

A late afternoon rainbow
hangs over Kilchurn castle
on Loch Awe in Scotland.
6th June, 1999

The Prince of Wales at the opening of the British Film Institute's IMAX cinema in Waterloo, London. The cinema shows 2D and 3D films on a screen over 20m high and 26m wide. Backed by a £15 million grant from the Arts Council of England's Lottery Fund, the £20 million purpose-built cinema immerses viewers in larger-than-life images and realistic digital sound.

11th June, 1999

Tim Henman dries off during his second round, Men's Singles match against Chris Woodruff.

24th June, 1999

James Dean Bradfield, lead
singer of the Manic Street
Preachers, performs on
the Pyramid Stage at the
Glastonbury Festival.
26th June, 1999

Glastonbury wristband
passes.
27th June, 1999

Concorde leads the Red
Arrows in a flypast at the
official opening of the
Scottish Parliament in
Edinburgh.
1st July, 1999

Greenpeace send a message to Tony Blair condemning recently departed shipments of weapons grade plutonium from Britain.
23rd July, 1999

Frankie Dettori leaps off his mount, 'Daylami', after winning the King George VI and Queen Elizabeth Diamond Stakes, at Ascot.
24th July, 1999

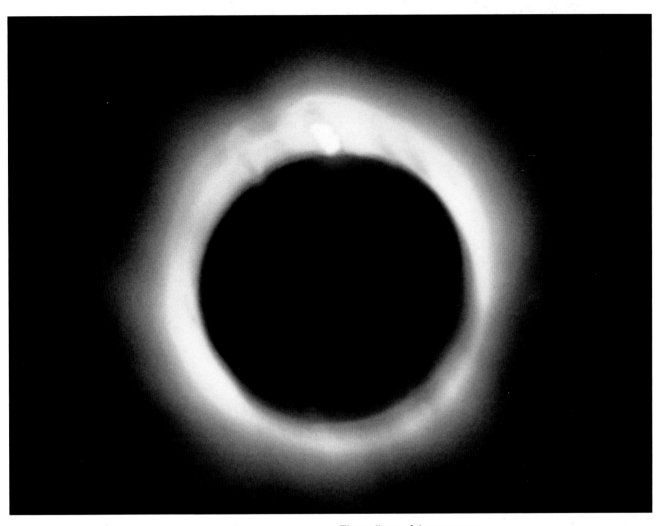

The eclipse of the sun over
Cornwall seen from an RAF
Hercules of 30 Squadron,
based at RAF Lyneham,
Wiltshire. Cloud cover
obscures the view from
watchers on the ground.
11th August, 1999

Manchester United's
David Beckham celebrates
their first goal against
Coventry City.
25th August, 1999

Michael Owen (on floor)
and the Liverpool fans
can't believe their bad luck
as Manchester United
goalkeeper Massimo Taibi
keeps another shot out
during an FA Premiership
football match.
11th September, 1999

Sadie Frost and her husband Jude Law making plaster casts of their hands at the premiere of their new film, 'Final Cut' at the Odeon West End, Leicester Square.
16th September, 1999

Reigning World Gurning Champion Peter Jackman gets in some last minute practice ahead of the defence of his title at the Egremont Crab Fair, near Whitehaven in Cumbria.
17th September, 1999

A Virgin light airship over the still horizontal Millennium Wheel (London Eye) in central London. The wheel is sponsored by British Airways. Virgin boss Richard Branson is taunting rivals BA with the 'British Airways Can't Get It Up' slogan. The Millennium Wheel was supposed to be lifted to its full 450ft height – three times taller than Tower Bridge – earlier that month but when the anchor clips holding the support cables started to buckle under the weight, the mission was aborted: **28th September, 1999**

Facing page: Rugby World Cup 99. A packed Lansdowne Road waits for Ireland to attempt a penalty kick against Australia. **10th October, 1999**

'Commuters from Hell' travel
on a rush hour tube train
to protest at the state of
London's Underground.
8th December, 1999

Channel Four's 'Big Breakfast' team announce they will celebrate the millennium with a massive eight and a half hour live special. Presented by (L-R) Richard Bacon, Sara Cox, Johnny Vaughan, Liza Tarbuck and Phil Gayle.
10th December, 1999

Dome organisers, the New
Millennium Experience
Company, are working
around the clock to get the
Millennium Dome finished on
time for the grand opening
by the Queen.
13th December, 1999

Prime Minister Tony
Blair travels on London
Underground's newly built
Jubilee Line extension,
en route to the Millennium
Dome in Greenwich.
14th December, 1999

Organisers present a preview of the Millennium Dome attractions to 14,000 people.
19th December, 1999

Facing page: A laser fired from the north side of the River Thames by the Prime Minister hits the Millennium Wheel at the start of New Year's Eve celebrations. Plans for passengers to use the new attraction have been scrapped after a last-minute safety hitch.
31st December, 1999

Revellers on the Victoria
Embankment, on the north
side of the River Thames.
31st December, 1999

Fireworks usher in the new
millennium at the stroke of
midnight in London.
1st January, 2000

WILLENHALL The **1990s** Britain in Pictures **299**

The Publishers gratefully acknowledge PA Photos, from whose extensive archive the photographs in this book have been selected. Personal copies of the photographs in this book, and many others, may be ordered online at www.prints.paphotos.com

For more information, please contact:

Ammonite Press

AE Publications Ltd. 166 High Street, Lewes, East Sussex, BN7 1XU, United Kingdom

Tel: 01273 488005 Fax: 01273 402866

www.ae-publications.com